D1212258

My Cookbook of

Baking

Laura and Jess Tilli

QEB Publishing

Difficulty rating

★ Easy peasy!

★★ Pretty simple

★★★ Getting tricky

★★★★ Chef's challenge

★★★★★ Super chef!

Always ask for an adult's help when you see these symbols:

An oven or hob is needed, or a hot item is handled.

An electrical appliance, such as an electric whisk is needed.

A sharp object, such as a knife or grater is needed.

Editor: Lauren Taylor
Designer: Andrew Crowson
Photography: Catrin Arwell
Additional recipe testing by Judith Furtig

Copyright © QEB Publishing 2012

Published in the United States by
QEB Publishing, Inc.
3 Wrigley, Suite A
Irvine, CA 92618

www.qed-publishing.co.uk

A CIP record for this book is available from the Library of Congress.

ISBN 978 1 60992 278 8

Printed in China

Serving sizes are approximations only.

All oven temperatures given are intended for fan assisted ovens. Standard conversions are given below:

Electric (fan) °C (°F)	Electric (no fan) °C (°F)	Gas mark
90 (190)	110 (230)	1/4
100 (200)	120 (250)	1/2
120 (250)	140 (285)	1
130 (265)	150 (300)	2
140 (285)	160 (320)	3
160 (320)	180 (350)	4
170 (325)	190 (375)	5
180 (350)	200 (400)	6
200 (400)	220 (425)	7
210 (410)	230 (450)	8
220 (245)	240 (465)	9

Contents

Techniques

Rubbing

Put your flour into a bowl with cold butter. Using your thumbs and fingertips, rub the butter into the flour, lifting your hands up and down to get lots of air into the mixture. Keep rubbing until the flour and butter have combined into crumbs. Be careful not to overrub as the mixture will become too sticky.

Rolling Pastry

Sprinkle some flour over a clean work surface and your rolling pin. Place the chilled pastry on top. Gently roll your rolling pin backwards and forwards over the pastry, pressing down slightly, until it stretches. Turn the pastry around and roll in the other direction so the pastry stretches into an even shape and thickness.

Whipping Cream

Pour the cream into a large bowl. With a whisk, beat the cream as fast as you can until it thickens. Be careful not to overwhip your cream or it will curdle.

Pan Greasing and Lining

Rub a small amount of butter or oil all over the inside of your pan. Draw around your pan onto a sheet of parchment paper. Cut out the paper circle and place it inside your greased pan.

Separating Eggs

Carefully crack an egg over a bowl and catch the yolk in your hand while letting the white run through your fingers. Put the yolk into a separate bowl.

Beating Eggs

Using a fork, beat the egg until the yolk is completely mixed into the white.

Whisking Egg Whites

Tip your whites into a large bowl and use an electric whisk to turn the whites into big white fluffy clouds. You can use a hand whisk too—it will just take a little longer, and more muscle power!

Folding

Very gently, move a metal spoon around the edge of your bowl then straight down the middle. Repeat until your ingredients are loosely combined. This technique is used to combine ingredients without stirring all the air and texture out of them.

Apple Coring and Dicing

Stand your apple up and carefully cut off each side until you are left with a square core to throw away. Chop the four sides you cut off into even cube-shaped chunks.

Piping Frosting

Place the nozzle on or inside the end of your piping bag. Roll the bag down until it is half the size. Spoon in your frosting. Twist the bag closed and squeeze the frosting right to the bottom and into the nozzle. Carefully squeeze the piping bag from the top to make the frosting pattern.

Melting

Place your ingredients in a saucepan. Over a low heat, gently stir your ingredients together until melted and combined. Take off the heat before they start to sizzle or burn.

Grating Cheese

With a large block of cheese in one hand and a grater in the other, move the block of cheese up and down over the grating holes, pressing quite firmly so that the cheese is shaved away. Don't try to grate very small pieces of cheese because it might hurt your fingers.

Coconut Squares with Jam

Rating ★

Ingredients:

12 tbsp unsalted butter
¾ cup granulated sugar
2 large eggs
2 tbsp Greek yogurt
1 ¼ cups all-purpose flour
1 tsp baking powder
¼ tsp salt
¼ cup strawberry jam,
½ cup desiccated coconut

Equipment:

1 wooden spoon
1 mixing bowl
1 9-inch square cake pan,
    greased and lined
1 butter knife

Preparation time: 20 minutes

Cooking time: 25 minutes

Makes: 24

1. Preheat oven to 325°F (170°C). With a wooden spoon, mix the butter and sugar together until creamy.

2. Add the eggs and yogurt. Mix until combined.

3. Add the flour, baking powder and salt and mix again.

4. Pour the mixture into the lined cake pan. Smooth it out to the corners.

Perfect to take on a picnic!

Tilli Tip

★ ★ ★

You can also halve the ingredients to make 12 squares.

5. Bake for 20-25 minutes, until golden. Once out of the oven, leave to cool in the pan.

6. Spread the jam over the sponge. Sprinkle the coconut over the jam.

7. When the sponge is completely cool, lift it out of the pan using the parchment paper. Cut into squares.

Banana and chocolate cupcakes

Rating ★

Ingredients:

10 tbsp butter
2/3 cup granulated sugar
2 large eggs
1 1/3 cups all-purpose flour
1 tsp baking powder
1/8 tsp salt
1/2 cup cocoa powder
1 mashed banana
Small handful of banana chips,
    to decorate

For the frosting:

1/4 cup butter
1/4 cup confectioners'
    sugar, sifted
1 tbsp cocoa

Equipment:

1 mixing bowl   1 sifter
1 whisk   1 piping bag
1 wooden spoon   and nozzle
1 tablespoon
1 teaspoon
1 muffin pan
12 cupcake liners
1 wire rack

Preparation time: 25 minutes

Cooking time: 20 minutes

Makes: 12

1. Preheat oven to 350°F (180°C). In a mixing bowl, mix together the softened butter and sugar until creamy. Add the eggs and whisk until smooth.

2. Using a wooden spoon, carefully mix the flour, baking powder, salt and cocoa into the egg mixture.

3. Fold in the mashed banana. Line the cupcake pan with the cupcake liners.

4. Using your tablespoon and teaspoon, place 2 tablespoons of batter into each cupcake liner.

Try This!

★ ★ ★

To add an extra burst of chocolate, top with chocolate chips.

You could use fresh banana slices instead of dried chips.

5. Bake for 20 minutes, until firm to touch. Leave to cool in the pan for a few minutes before transferring them to a wire rack to cool completely.

6. To make the frosting, mix all the frosting ingredients together until smooth. Transfer the mixture into a piping bag.

7. Pipe the frosting into swirly waves on top of each cupcake. Top with the banana chips.

Strawberry Jam Shortbread Cookies

Rating

Ingredients:
1 cup (2 sticks) butter
²/₃ cup confectioners' sugar
1 tsp vanilla extract
1 ¼ cups all-purpose flour
5 tbsp cornstarch
½ cup good quality
   strawberry jam

Equipment:
1 mixing bowl
1 wooden spoon
1 sifter
2 baking trays, greased and lined
1 wire rack

Preparation time: 20 minutes

Cooking time: 15 minutes

Makes: 12

1. Preheat oven to 350°F (180°C). Mix together the butter, sugar and vanilla extract until creamy.

2. Sift the flour and cornstarch into the butter mixture. Mix well until you have a smooth dough.

Tilli Tip

★ ★ ★

If your dough feels too sticky, dust your hands with a little flour before rolling the balls.

You can use any flavor of jam you like!

3. Using your hands, roll the dough into 24 small balls. Space them out the baking trays. Flatten each ball slightly with your fingers.

4. Bake for 12-15 minutes, until the shortbread is golden brown. Transfer the shortbread to a wire rack to cool completely.

5. Sandwich pairs of the shortbread together with the strawberry jam.

Popping Candy Muffins

Rating ★★★

Ingredients:

10 tbsp unsalted butter
$2/3$ cup granulated sugar
2 large eggs
1 $1/2$ cups all-purpose flour
1 tsp baking powder
$1/8$ tsp salt
2 tsp vanilla extract
2 packets popping candy, 1 for
    batter, 1 for topping

For the frosting:

1 $3/4$ cups confectioners'
    sugar sifted
12 tbsp (1 $1/2$ sticks)
    unsalted butter
1 tsp vanilla extract

Equipment:

1 mixing bowl   1 teaspoon
1 wooden spoon   1 tablespoon
1 whisk   1 piping bag
1 muffin pan   and nozzle
12 cupcake liners
1 wire rack

Preparation time: 25 minutes

Cooking time: 20 minutes

Makes: 12

1. Preheat oven to 350°F (180°C). Mix together the butter and sugar using a wooden spoon.

2. Whisk the two eggs into the butter mixture. Stir in the flour, baking powder, salt and vanilla extract and one pack of popping candy. Line the muffin pan with the cupcake liners.

3. Using a teaspoon and tablespoon, place 2 tablespoons of mixture into each liner.

4. Bake for 20 minutes, until the muffins are golden brown.

The popping candy will really surprise your friends!

5. Leave the muffins in the pan to cool for a few minutes. Transfer to a wire rack to cool completely.

6. To make the frosting, mix together the confectioners' sugar and butter. Stir in the vanilla extract and transfer the mixture to a piping bag.

7. Pipe a small amount of frosting on top of each muffin. Sprinkle with popping candy before the frosting dries.

Sausage and Apple Pastry Puffs

Rating ★ ★

Ingredients:

1 sheet puff pastry, thawed
1 pound bulk pork sausage
1 apple, finely chopped
1 medium onion,
   finely chopped
2 cloves garlic, crushed
1 large egg, beaten
Salt and pepper
Ketchup, for dipping

Equipment:

1 mixing bowl
1 wooden spoon
1 pastry brush
1 butter knife
1 baking tray, greased and lined

Preparation time: 30 minutes

Cooking time: 25 minutes

Makes: 12

1. Preheat oven to 350°F (180°C). Unroll the pastry onto a flat, clean surface.

2. In a large bowl, mix together the sausage meat, apple, onion, garlic and salt and pepper.

3. With your hands, scoop out the sausage mixture and place onto the pastry, making a long sausage shape down the middle.

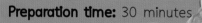

14

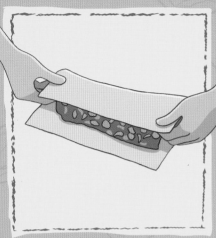

4. With a pastry brush or your fingers, brush the beaten egg down both sides of the pastry. Fold the pastry over the sausage meat and press down to firmly to seal.

5. Slice the sausage into 1 inch slices, and make a slit in the top of each one with a butter knife.

6. Place the sausage rolls onto your lined baking tray. Brush each one with beaten egg. Bake for 25 minutes, until golden brown.

7. Leave to cool slightly before dipping in ketchup and gobbling up!

Try This!
★ ★ ★

Instead of apple, you could try adding rosemary and sage.

Dipping the puffs in mustard will be just as yummy!

Triple-Cheese Muffins

Rating ★★

Ingredients:

6 tbsp unsalted butter
2 tbsp olive oil
½ cup bread crumbs
3 large eggs
1 ⅔ cups all-purpose flour
1 ½ tsp baking powder
¼ tsp salt
¼ cup water
2 oz. Cheddar cheese, grated
2 oz. crumbled feta cheese
Small handful of Parmesan
   cheese, grated
Small handful of pumpkin seeds
Salt and pepper

Equipment:

1 mixing bowl
1 wooden spoon
1 whisk
1 large measuring cup
1 muffin pan
12 cupcake liners
1 teaspoon
1 tablespoon
1 wire rack

Preparation time: 20 minutes

Cooking time: 25 minutes

Makes: 12

1. Preheat oven to 350°F (180°C). In your bowl, mix together the butter, oil and breadcrumbs.

2. Whisk the eggs and a pinch of salt and pepper into the breadcrumb mixture.

3. Add the flour, baking powder, salt and baking powder to the bowl. Mix until smooth. Slowly stir in the water.

Seeds are a healthy snack!

4. Stir in the grated Cheddar and crumbled feta. Line the muffin pan with the liners.

5. Using the tablespoon and teaspoon, carefully fill each muffin cup to about halfway. Sprinkle each with Parmesan cheese and pumpkin seeds. Bake for about 25 minutes, until the muffins have risen and are golden brown.

6. Leave to cool slightly in their pan, then transfer to a wire rack. They are delicious eaten while still warm!

Try This!
★ ★ ★

You can use any cheese you like—why not try crumbled Stilton?

Mini Sausage Batter Bites

Rating ★

Ingredients:

3 large eggs (cracked into a large measuring cup)
Equal parts of all-purpose flour to the eggs
Equal parts of milk to the eggs
24 small/cocktail sausages
12 tsp vegetable oil, plus extra for frying
Salt and pepper
Ketchup or mustard, to serve

Equipment:

1 mixing bowl
1 fine mesh strainer
1 whisk
1 frying pan
1 (12-cup) muffin pan
1 teaspoon
1 small jug

Preparation time: 25 minutes

Cooking time: 20 minutes

Makes: 12

1. Preheat oven to 400°F (200°C). Whisk together the eggs, flour, milk and salt and pepper, until you have a smooth batter. Strain the mixture through a fine mesh strainer if you have any lumps.

2. Gently fry the sausages in a little vegetable oil until they are browned.

3. Place two sausages into each muffin cup, with a teaspoon of oil in each hole. Heat in the oven for 5 minutes, until the oil is hot.

Tilli Tip

★ ★ ★

It is important to heat the oil before adding the batter so it puffs up well and is crisp.

Perfect as a party snack!

4. Carefully remove the pan from the oven. Using the jug, pour the batter into each muffin cup, so that the sausages are slightly covered.

5. Return to the oven for about 12 minutes, until the batter has puffed up and is golden brown.

6. Serve warm with ketchup or mustard for dipping—or both!

Toffee Apple Layer Cake

Rating ⭐

Ingredients:
12 tbsp (1 ½ sticks) unsalted butter
1 cup packed light brown sugar
3 large eggs
1 ¼ cups all-purpose flour
2 tsp baking powder
¼ tsp salt
3 apples, peeled, cored, and diced
½ cup dark brown sugar
1 cup heavy cream, whipped
Mini fudge or soft toffee pieces

Equipment:
1 mixing bowl   1 wire rack
1 wooden spoon
2 spring-bottom cake pans, greased and lined

Preparation time: 30 minutes

Cooking time: 25 minutes

Makes: 12

1. Preheat oven to 350°F (180°C). Mix together the butter and light brown sugar until creamy.

You could try pears instead of apples.

2. Mix the eggs, flour and baking powder and salt into the butter mixture until you have a smooth mixture.

3. Divide the mixture between the two lined cake pans and scatter the diced apple over the top.

4. Sprinkle the mixture with the dark brown sugar. Bake for 35 minutes, until golden brown.

5. Leave the cakes to cool in their pans for 5 minutes. Turn out onto a wire rack to cool completely.

6. Gently fold your mini fudge or toffee pieces into the whipped cream. Sandwich your cakes together with the cream.

Try This!
★ ★ ★

You could replace the whipped cream filling with a thin layer of apple sauce for a lighter, fruitier taste.

Chocolate Bread and Butter Pudding

Rating ★ ★

Ingredients:

8 slices of 2-day-old bread, buttered
½ jar chocolate spread
½ cup chocolate chips
½ cup raisins
2 large eggs
1 cup milk
2 tbsp sugar
Whipped cream, to serve (optional)

Equipment:

1 butter knife
1 medium casserole dish or loaf pan, greased and lined
1 mixing bowl
1 whisk

Preparation time: 15 minutes

Cooking time: 40 minutes

Serves: 4–6

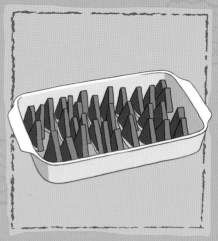

1. Preheat oven to 350°F (180°C). Spread each slice of buttered bread with a generous layer of chocolate spread, and cut into four triangles.

2. Layer the triangles in the casserole dish with the points facing up.

3. Sprinkle over the chocolate chips and raisins.

4. In a mixing bowl, whisk together the eggs and milk. Pour the egg mixture all over the chocolate bread.

5. Sprinkle the sugar over the mixture and bake for 40 minutes, until the pudding has set and the bread points are golden brown.

Try This!

★ ★ ★

You could add fresh banana slices between the bread layers too!

6. Cut into slices and serve with whipped cream for a delicious treat!

Any kind of dried fruit will work well in this pudding.

Very Berry Crumble

Rating ★★★

Ingredients:

1 pint mixed berries, fresh
   or frozen
¼ cup granulated sugar
1 ¼ cups all-purpose flour
6 tbsp unsalted butter
½ cup packed light brown sugar
½ cup rolled oats, uncooked
Small handful of pumpkin seeds

Equipment:

1 saucepan
1 wooden spoon
1 mixing bowl
1 large ovenproof casserole dish

Preparation time: 30 minutes

Cooking time: 25 minutes

Makes: 12

1. Preheat oven to 350°F (180°C). Gently heat the berries and granulated sugar in a saucepan until slightly soft. If using fresh berries, add a little water to the pan. Place the mixture into the pie dish.

2. For the crumble topping, gently rub the flour and butter in a bowl, using your fingertips, until the mixture looks like breadcrumbs.

3. Carefully mix the brown sugar and oats into the crumble mixture.

Seeds give the topping a delicious crunch!

Tilli Tip

★ ★ ★

Try serving this warm with whipped cream or vanilla ice cream.

4. Sprinkle the crumble mixture over the berries. Scatter the pumpkin seeds over the crumble.

5. Bake for 30 minutes, until the crumble is golden and the berries are bubbling!

Raspberry and Almond Puff Pancake

Rating ★★

Ingredients:

3 tbsp vegetable oil
3 large eggs (cracked
    into a large measuring cup)
Equal amounts of all-purpose
    flour to the eggs
Equal amounts of milk to
    the eggs
3 tbsp granulated
¾ cups raspberries
½ cup flaked almonds
Confectioners' sugar, to dust
Whipped cream or ice cream,
    to serve (optional)

Equipment:

1 ovenproof shallow dish
1 mixing bowl
1 whisk

Preparation time: 10 minutes

Cooking time: 30 minutes

Serves: 6

1. Preheat oven to 350°F (180°C). Pour the oil into the ovenproof dish, and heat in the oven for 5 minutes.

2. In a bowl, whisk together the eggs, flour, milk and sugar.

3. Remove dish from the oven, and transfer the batter into the dish.

4. Scatter the raspberries and almonds on top . Return to the oven for 25 minutes, until the pan bake is puffy and golden.

Almonds and raspberries taste wonderful together!

5. Dust with confectioners' sugar and serve warm with whipped cream or ice cream.

Tilli Tip
★ ★ ★

Be extremely careful when pouring the batter into the hot oil in step 3, as the oil may spit.

The Best Baked Potatoes

Rating ★ ★

Ingredients:
4 large russet potatoes
½ can baked beans
2 sprigs onions, cut into
　　small pieces
4 oz. Cheddar cheese, grated
3 tbsp butter, softened
Salt and pepper

Equipment:
1 fork
2 mixing bowls
1 wooden spoon
1 butter knife
1 spoon
1 baking tray

Preparation time: 20 minutes

Cooking time: 30 minutes

Serves: 4–8

1. Preheat oven to 400°F
(200°C). Prick the potatoes
with a fork and cook them
in the microwave for about
9 minutes, until soft. Leave
to cool.

2. Pour the baked beans into
a mixing bowl. Add the onions,
a pinch of salt and pepper,
and half the grated cheese.
Mix well.

3. Cut each potato in
half and carefully scoop
out most of the potato
from the skin into a
small bowl. Keep the
skins to one side.

★ ★ ★

The potatoes may need more or less time in the microwave, depending on how big they are.

Great for a delicious lunch!

4. Add the potato and butter to the bowl with the other ingredients. Mix well.

5. Using a spoon, fill the cooled potato skins with the cheesy bean and potato mixture. Place on a baking tray.

6. Sprinkle the rest of the grated cheese on top of the potatoes. Bake for 20 minutes, until golden brown.

Garlicky Mushroom Pasta Bake

Rating ★ ★ ★

Ingredients:

2 tbsp olive oil
1 small onion, finely chopped
2 cloves of garlic, finely chopped
5 oz. button mushrooms,
   cleaned and sliced
2 tbsp fresh chopped parsley
8 oz. dried spiral-shaped pasta
3 oz. cream cheese
½ cup grated Cheddar cheese,
Salt and pepper

Equipment:

1 frying pan
1 wooden spoon
1 saucepan
1 colander
1 spoon
1 ovenproof dish

Preparation time: 20 minutes

Cooking time: 25 minutes

Serves: 4–6

1. Preheat oven to 350°F (180°C). In your frying pan, gently heat the olive oil. Add the onion and cook gently for 5 minutes, until soft

2. Add the garlic and mushrooms. Cook for a further 6-8 minutes. Add the parsley and a pinch of salt and pepper. Turn off the heat.

3. In the saucepan, cook the pasta in boiling water for 5 minutes. Turn off the heat. Drain well and return the pasta to the saucepan. The pasta should still be a little hard at this stage.

4. Add the cream cheese to the cooked pasta. Stir well. Add the garlicky mushroom mixture.

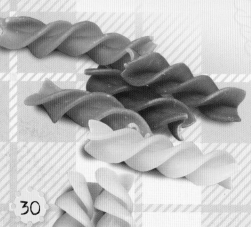

Try This!
★ ★ ★

Try using different types of cheeses for a different taste-how about Monterey Jack or feta?

5. Transfer the pasta mixture into an ovenproof dish. Sprinkle with the cheese. Bake in the oven for 25 minutes, until the cheese is golden and bubbling.

Spinach and Feta Pie

Rating ★ ★ ★

Ingredients:

Olive oil, for frying and brushing
1 small onion, finely chopped
2 leeks, washed and chopped
8 oz. baby spinach leaves
1 package ready-made
   filo pastry
7 oz. feta cheese
1 large egg, beaten
Small handful of poppy seeds
Salt and pepper

Equipment:

1 teaspoon
1 large saucepan with lid
1 wooden spoon
1 butter knife
1 large tart pan with
   removable bottom
1 pastry brush
1 bowl

Preparation time: 30 minutes

Cooking time: 55 minutes

Serves: 6–8

1. Preheat oven to 400°F (200°C). Add a teaspoon of olive oil to your saucepan and heat gently.

2. Add the chopped onions and leeks. Cook for about 10 minutes, until soft and slightly golden.

3. Add the spinach and a pinch of salt and pepper. Cover and turn off the heat.

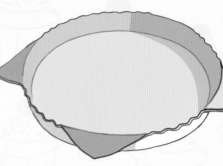

4. Unroll the filo pastry. Cut a strip off the top so that you have a square shape. Peel off one layer and place it on the greased pan, so it hangs over the edges of the pan. Brush evenly with olive oil, using a pastry brush.

5. Peel off another layer of pastry. Place on top of the first layer, turning the pan so the layers form a star pattern. Brush with oil. Repeat with another three layers of pastry.

6. Crumble the feta cheese into a bowl. Add the onion mixture to the feta and mix well. Stir the egg into this cheesy onion mixture.

7. Pour the mixture into the pastry-lined pan. Fold the overhanging pastry into the middle. You may need to add a couple of extra scrunched-up sheets of pastry to fill any gaps.

8. Drizzle the pie with olive oil and sprinkle with poppy seeds. Bake for 45 minutes, until golden brown.

Tilli Tip
★ ★ ★
You can use your fingertips to spread the oil instead of a pastry brush, but be careful not to tear the pastry!

Apricot Jam Tarts

Rating ⭐⭐

Ingredients:
²⁄₃ cup all-purpose flour, plus
    extra for dusting
7 tbsp cold butter
3 tbsp water
½ cup good-quality apricot jam

Equipment:
1 mixing bowl
1 12-cup muffin pan
1 metal spoon
Plastic wrap
1 rolling pin
1 pastry cutter (slightly bigger
    than the muffin pan holes)
1 teaspoon

Preparation time: 45 minutes

Cooking time: 25 minutes

Makes: 12

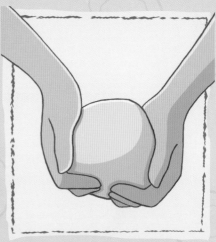

1. Preheat oven to 350°F (180°C). Using your fingertips, rub the flour and butter together until it looks like breadcrumbs.

2. Fold in the water with a metal spoon, until the mixture comes together. Using your hands, shape the dough into a ball, cover with plastic wrap and put in the refrigerator for 30 minutes.

Great for a summer picnic!

Tilli Tip
★ ★ ★
You can use any flavor of jam for this recipe, or even marmalade or lemon curd!

3. With your rolling pin, roll out the pastry on a floured surface until it's ¼ in (2 cm) thick.

4. Cut out 12 circles with your pastry cutter. Put the circles in the cups of your muffin pan, squashing them down to the bottom.

5. Place a teaspoon of apricot jam into each pastry circle. Bake for 25 minutes, until the pastry is golden brown. The jam will be very hot, so wait for them to cool slightly before digging in!

35

Baked Cheese with Toast

Rating ★ ★

Ingredients:

1 small wheel of soft cheese
    with rind (e.g. Camembert)
4 cherry tomatoes, halved
6 small sprigs fresh rosemary
1 small baguette
Olive oil
Sea salt

Equipment:

Baking tray, lined
Butter knife
Chopping board
Bread knife

Preparation time: 10 minutes

Cooking time: 20 minutes

Serves: 12

1. Preheat oven to 350°F (180°C). Place the cheese in the middle of the baking tray. Make 12 small slits in the top with your butter knife.

2. Push half a cherry tomato and a sprig of rosemary into each slit.

3. Carefully cut your baguette into small slices. Arrange them around your cheese on the baking tray.

Try This!

★ ★ ★

If you don't like rosemary, you could swap it for small slices of garlic or some fresh basil.

This looks amazing on a buffet table!

4. Drizzle the bread with olive oil and sprinkle with a little sea salt. Bake for 20 minutes, until the cheese is melted and bubbling.

5. Cut into the top of the cheese and dip the pieces of toast in.

Chocolate Anything Cookies

Rating ★ ★ ★

Ingredients:

5 tbsp unsalted butter, softened
1/3 cup granulated sugar
1 large egg
2/3 cup all-purpose flour
1 tsp baking powder
1/4 tsp salt
1/3 cup of your favorite chocolate treat, such as chocolate raisins or chips

Equipment:

1 mixing bowl
1 wooden spoon
2 spoons
1 baking tray, greased and lined
1 wire rack

Preparation time: 15 minutes

Cooking time: 15 minutes

Makes: 24

1. Preheat oven to 350°F (180°C). Using a wooden spoon, mix the butter and sugar together until creamy.

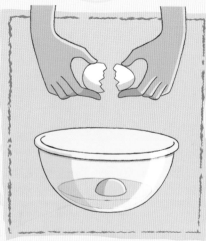

2. Add the egg and stir well.

3. Add the flour, baking powder, salt and chocolate chips, raisins or buttons to the egg mixture. Mix well until you have a smooth mixture.

4. Using 2 spoons, place large spoonfuls of dough 2 inches (5 cm) apart on your baking tray.

5. Bake for 15 minutes, until golden brown. Leave to cool on the tray for a few minutes,

6. Transfer your cookies onto a wire rack to cool completely.

Add a mixture of white and milk chocolate for a yummy alternative!

Tilli Tip
⭐ ⭐ ⭐

Don't put spoonfuls of dough too close to each other on the baking tray or you'll end up with one big cookie!

Peanut Butter Baked Bananas

Rating ⭐

Ingredients:
4 ripe bananas
4 tbsp peanut butter
1 small package
   chocolate chips
Confectioners' sugar, to dust

Equipment:
1 butter knife
1 tablespoon
Aluminum foil
1 baking tray

Preparation time: 10 minutes

Cooking time: 30 minutes

Makes: 4

1. Preheat oven to 350°F (180°C). Carefully make a split down the middle of each banana with a butter knife. Be careful not to chop them in half.

2. Place a tablespoon of peanut butter inside each banana, smoothing it right down to the ends.

3. Place the chocolate chips into the peanut butter. Wrap the bananas in aluminum foil.

You can use crunchy or smooth peanut butter.

4. Place the bananas on a baking tray and bake for 30 minutes.

5. Leave to cool slightly, then unwrap. Dust with confectioners' sugar and eat with a spoon.

Pesto Pizza

Rating ★★★

Ingredients:

1 sheet of puff pastry, thawed
All-purpose flour, for dusting
2 tbsp tomato purée
½ can chopped tomatoes
3 oz. buffalo mozzarella
3 tbsp green pesto
1 handful Cheddar
   cheese, grated
2 tbsp olive oil
1 large egg, beaten
Basil leaves, to garnish
Salt and pepper

Equipment:

1 rolling pin
1 baking tray
1 spoon
1 teaspoon
1 pastry brush

Preparation time: 30 minutes

Cooking time: 15 minutes

Serves: 6–8

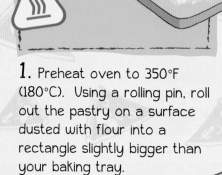

1. Preheat oven to 350°F (180°C). Using a rolling pin, roll out the pastry on a surface dusted with flour into a rectangle slightly bigger than your baking tray.

2. Lay the pastry onto the tray. With your hands, fold in the sides to create a ½ inch (1 ½ cm) border all the way around.

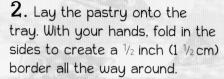

Try This!
★★★
You can add whatever toppings you like to this pizza. Why not try ham and sweet corn?

42

*Great to share
with friends at
a sleepover!*

5. Brush all four edges of
the pizza with the beaten
egg. Drizzle with olive oil
and sprinkle on a little salt
and pepper. Bake for 15
minutes, until the pastry is
golden brown. Scatter the
basil leaves over the top
before serving.

*The olive oil will
stop the pizza from
drying out
while baking.*

3. With the back of a spoon,
spread the tomato purée over
the pastry. Repeat with the
canned tomatoes. Tear up the
mozzarella into chunks and
sprinkle over the pizza.

4. With a teaspoon, dot
the pesto all over the pizza.
Sprinkle over the cheese.

Twisty Cheese Sticks

Rating ★★★

Ingredients:
1 sheet of puff pastry, thawed
4 tbsp milk
¼ cup Parmesan cheese, grated
¼ cup Cheddar cheese, grated

Equipment:
1 pastry brush
1 butter knife
1 baking tray, greased and lined
1 slotted spatula

Preparation time: 15 minutes

Cooking time: 20 minutes

Makes: 12

1. Preheat oven to 350°F (180°C). Place the pastry sheet onto a flat, clean surface.

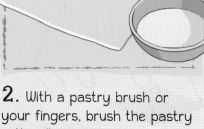

2. With a pastry brush or your fingers, brush the pastry with milk.

Tilli Tip
★ ★ ★

After you've twisted your pastry fingers in step 4, squeeze the ends slightly to stop them unravelling.

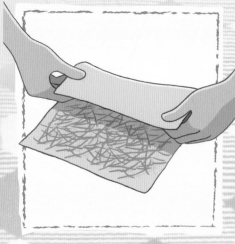

3. Sprinkle over both cheeses and fold the pastry in half. Slice the pastry into 12 fingers.

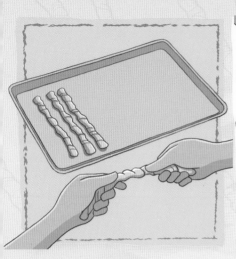

4. Carefully twist each pastry finger, then place onto the baking tray.

5. Brush the twists with more milk. Bake for 15–20 minutes, until the pastry is golden and the cheese is bubbling.

6. Leave to cool on the tray. Transfer to a serving dish using a spatula.

Perfect for sharing with friends!

All-In-One Breakfast Bake

Rating ★ ★ ★

Ingredients:
1 tbsp olive oil
2 sausage links
2 slices of bacon
5 mushrooms, halved
½ can tomatoes
2 large eggs
Chopped chives, to garnish
Buttered toast, to serve

Equipment:
1 frying pan
1 shallow ovenproof dish
1 wooden spoon

Preparation time: 15 minutes

Cooking time: 20 minutes

Serves: 2

1. Preheat oven to 350°F (180°C). Heat the oil in the frying pan and gently fry the sausages and bacon until slightly browned. Add the mushrooms for the final 2 minutes of cooking time.

2. Transfer the sausages and mushrooms into a casserole dish. Pour over the tomatoes. Make two hollows in the mixture with a spoon and break an egg into each hollow.

3. Bake for 20 minutes, until the eggs are cooked through.

4. Sprinkle with chives. Serve with hot buttered toast.

Perfect for a lazy weekend breakfast!

Try This!

★ ★ ★

Use vegetarian sausages and bacon for a veggie version. Check the cooking instructions first.

Cheesy Baked Tomatoes

Rating ★★

Ingredients:
6 large tomatoes
3 oz. grated mozzarella
1 green pepper, chopped into
　　small chunks
1 small can sweet corn
¼ cup chopped fresh parsley
2 tbsp olive oil, plus
　　extra to drizzle
Salt and pepper

Equipment:
1 sharp knife
1 teaspoon
1 mixing bowl
1 wooden spoon
1 baking tray, lined

Preparation time: 15 minutes

Cooking time: 20 minutes

Serves: 6

1. Preheat oven to 400°F (200°C). Carefully slice the top off each tomato and place the tops to one side.

2. Using a teaspoon, scoop out the insides of the tomatoes and discard.

3. In a mixing bowl, add the cheese, chopped pepper, sweetcorn, parsley, olive oil and a pinch of salt and pepper. Stir well.

4. Using the teaspoon, fill the tomatoes with the mixture. Place the tomatoes on the baking tray and replace their tops.

5. Drizzle with olive oil and bake for 20 minutes, until soft and smelling delicious!

You can stuff the tomatoes with any vegetables you like!

Tilli Tip

★ ★ ★

Beefsteak tomatoes are the biggest and are perfect for this recipe.

Cinnamon Raisin Cookies

Rating ★★

Ingredients:

5 tbsp unsalted butter
1/3 cup granulated sugar
1 large egg
2/3 cup all-purpose flour
1/2 tsp baking powder
1/8 tsp salt
1 cup uncooked, old-fashioned rolled oats
1/2 cup raisins
1 tsp cinnamon

Equipment:

1 mixing bowl   1 wire rack
1 wooden spoon
2 spoon
1 baking tray, greased and lined

Preparation time: 20 minutes

Cooking time: 15 minutes

Makes: 24

1. Preheat oven to 350°F (180°C). Using a wooden spoon, mix the butter and sugar together until creamy.

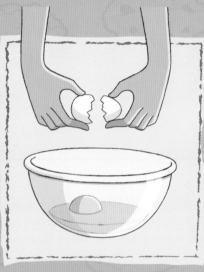

2. Add the egg to the butter mixture and stir well.

3. Add the flour, baking powder, salt, oats, raisins and cinnamon. Mix well until you have a smooth mixture.

4. Using 2 spoons, place big spoonfuls of dough 2 in. (5 cm) apart on a baking tray.

Try This!

★ ★ ★

Add half a teaspoon of ground ginger for a really spicy flavor!

5. Bake for 12–15 minutes, until the cookies are golden brown. Leave to cool on the tray for a few minutes.

6. Transfer the cookies to a wire rack to cool.

Oats are a really healthy addition to cookies.

Lumpy-Bumpy Shortbread

Rating ★★

Ingredients:

7 tbsp cold butter
¼ cup granulated sugar
1 tsp vanilla extract
1 ¼ cups all-purpose flour, plus
    extra to dust
¼ cup chocolate chips
¼ cup candied cherries, chopped
Handful of pumpkin seeds
Confectioners' sugar, to dust
Sprinkles, to decorate

Equipment:

1 mixing bowl
1 wooden spoon
1 rolling pin
1 baking tray, greased and lined
1 butter knife
1 wire rack

Preparation time: 50 minutes

Cooking time: 20 minutes

Makes: 24

1. Preheat oven to 350°F (180°C). Mix the butter, sugar and vanilla together until creamy.

2. Stir in the flour until the mixture is smooth and forms a dough.

3. Add the chocolate chips, cherries and seeds. Mix well.

These are full of interesting textures!

4. Turn the dough out onto a clean, floured work surface and gently roll out until it's ½ inch (1 ½ cm) thick.

5. Cut the dough into chunky bars. Place them onto a baking tray. Dust with confectioners' sugar and put the tray in the refrigerator for 30 minutes.

6. Bake for 15-20 minutes, until the cookies are lightly golden. Scatter with sprinkles, Transfer onto a wire rack to cool.

Tilli Tip

★ ★ ★

Add the sprinkles as soon as the shortbread leaves the oven—they will stick in the soft dough.

Giant Glitter Meringues

Rating ★ ★ ★

Ingredients:
4 large egg whites
1 cup granulated sugar
Red food coloring
Fine edible glitter, to sprinkle

Equipment:
1 electric whisk or
    standing mixer
1 extra-clean mixing
    bowl (not plastic)
1 metal spoon
2 tablespoons
1 baking tray, greased and lined

Preparation time: 4+ hours

Cooking time: 30 minutes

Serves: 8

1. Preheat oven to 300°F (150°C). Begin to whisk the egg whites in a mixing bowl with an electric whisk or a standing mixer.

2. Slowly add the sugar, a spoonful at a time. Keep whisking until the whites form a stiff mixture with no runny whites at the bottom of the bowl. Be careful not to overwhisk.

54

These will look fantastic at a glitzy party!

3. Add a couple of drops of food coloring and swirl in gently with a metal spoon, creating a marbled effect. Be careful not to lose volume.

4. Using two spoons, place big dollops of the meringue batter evenly over the lined baking tray, leaving space between each one.

5. Bake for 30 minutes. Turn off the oven and leave the meringues to dry in the oven for at least four hours, or preferably overnight. Sprinkle over the glitter to serve.

Really Sticky Oat Bars

Rating ★★

Ingredients:
6 tbsp butter
2 tbsp golden syrup
⅓ cup packed dark brown sugar
2 ½ cups uncooked, old-fashioned rolled oats
½ cup desiccated coconut

Equipment:
1 saucepan
1 wooden spoon
1 baking tray, greased and lined
1 butter knife

Preparation time: 15 minutes

Cooking time: 25 minutes

Makes: 24

1. Preheat oven to 350°F (180°C). In a saucepan, over a low heat, gently melt together the butter, syrup and sugar.

2. Turn off the heat. Add the oats and coconut. Mix well using a wooden spoon.

Classic oat bars with a twist of coconut!

Tilli Tip

If you dip the spoon in hot water before dipping in the syrup, it will be much easier to handle.

3. Pour the mixture onto the baking tray. Flatten out to the edges.

4. Bake for 25 minutes, until golden.

5. Using a butter knife, carefully cut the bars into squares. Leave to cool in the tray before removing and dividing into portions.

Lemon and Poppy Seed Cake

Ingredients:

12 tbsp (1 ½ sticks) unsalted butter
1 cup granulated sugar, plus extra to sprinkle
3 large eggs
1 ½ cups all-purpose flour
2 tsp baking powder
½ tsp salt
2 tsp baking powder
Juice and zest of 1 lemon
2 tbsp poppy seeds

Equipment:

1 mixing bowl   1 spoon
1 wooden spoon   1 butter knife
1 9-inch square baking
   pan, greased and lined
1 toothpick
1 wire rack

Preparation time: 15 minutes

Cooking time: 35 minutes

Makes: 24

1. Preheat oven to 350°F (180°C). Using a wooden spoon, mix together the butter and sugar until creamy.

2. Add the eggs to the butter mixture. Mix well.

3. Stir in the flour, baking powder, salt, lemon juice, lemon zest and poppyseeds. Pour the batter into a cake pan and smooth to the edges.

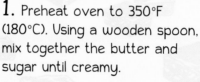

4. Bake for 35 minutes, until a toothpick inserted in the middle comes out clean.

5. Cool in the pan for 5 minutes. Transfer to a wire rack to cool completely. Sprinkle over a generous amount of sugar.

6. Slice into delicious squares before serving.

A light and refreshing snack for a summer's day!

Try This!

Try drizzling this cake with a little lemon-flavored frosting for an extra tangy finish!

Ham and Sweet Corn Quiche

Rating ★★

Ingredients:

1 (9-inch) readymade pie crust
½ onion, finely chopped
1 tbsp olive oil
3 large eggs
4 slices ham, chopped into
    small pieces
1 small can sweet corn
½ cup heavy cream mixed
    with ½ cup sour cream
½ cup grated Cheddar cheese
Salt and pepper

Equipment:

1 round tart pan with
    removable bottom
1 pair scissors
1 fork
1 frying pan
1 wooden spoon
1 mixing bowl
1 whisk

Preparation time: 30 minutes

Cooking time: 25 minutes

Serves: 8–10

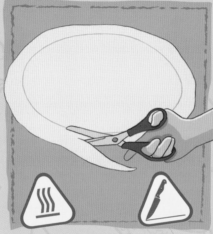

1. Preheat oven to 350°F (180°C). Unroll the pie crust and lay it over the tart pan. Use scissors to cut the crust to fit, leaving a ½ inch overhang all the way around. Press the dough into the pan.

2. With a fork, prick holes all over the pastry and bake for 20 minutes. The pastry shouldn't turn golden yet.

3. In a frying pan, gently fry the onion in the olive oil over a low heat, until soft. Leave to cool.

4. In a bowl, whisk together the eggs with a pinch of salt and pepper. Stir in the ham, sweetcorn, onions, and cream mix Pour into the pastry shell.

Tilli Tip

★ ★ ★

This quiche is delicious cold. Why not wrap slices up in parchment paper for a picnic in the park?

Serve with a salad for a delicious lunch.

5. Sprinkle the quiche with the grated cheese and bake for 25 minutes, until the cheese is bubbling and the pastry is golden.

Toasty Mini Ham and Cheese Bites

Rating ★ ★ ★

Ingredients:

12 slices brown bread
Butter, to spread
6 slices ham
1 cup grated Cheddar cheese
Ketchup, to spread
2 large eggs, beaten

Equipment:

1 butter knife
1 small, round cookie cutter
1 baking tray, lined and greased
1 small bowl

Preparation time: 20 minutes

Cooking time: 20 minutes

Makes: 12

1. Preheat oven to 350°F (180°C). Spread a thin layer of butter onto each slice of bread.

2. On six of the slices, place a slice of ham and a small handful of grated cheese.

Leave out the ham for a vegetarian version.

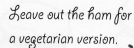

3. On the remaining 6 slices, spread a small amount of ketchup. Make into 6 sandwiches with the cheesy ham slices.

Tilli Tip

★ ★ ★

If you don't have a cookie cutter, use a small upside down water glass. You'll have to push down quite firmly.

4. Using the cookie cutter, cut out two circles from each sandwich.

5. Dip each circle into the beaten egg and place on the baking tray.

6. Bake the mini sandwiches for 20 minutes, until crisp. These can be enjoyed hot or cold.

Index